PLAY
SOCCER

PLAY SOCCER

Coach and Technical Adviser Mark Drabwell
Written by Catherine Saunders
Photography by Russell Sadur

Contents

Introduction

You probably already know the basics of soccer—it is a game played between two teams of eleven players and the object is to score more goals than the other team. Sounds simple! But do you really know how to play the game like a pro? Do you know a driven pass from a swerve shot or a Cruyff turn from a drag back? Well, it's time to get your cleats on and find out!

The Coach

All the techniques and skills in this book are performed under the supervision of FA-qualified coach Mark Drabwell. Mark holds a UEFA A License Diploma and is a Staff Coach for the English FA. He is committed to teaching the correct techniques and skills from an early age and regularly coaches children of all ages and abilities.

To get the most out of this book, read each page carefully. Make sure that you check out the step-by-step skills and helpful tips. Then get out there and practice! The more you practice, the better you will become.

HISTORY

As you will see when you turn the page, uniforms have changed a lot since 1881!

Although a form of soccer can be traced as far back as the Ancient Chinese, Greek, and Roman civilizations, the modern game originated nearly 150 years ago in England. In 1863, association football (what we now call soccer) and rugby football became two separate games. Since then, soccer as has spread all over the world. Today, the game's governing body, FIFA (Fédération Internationale de Football Association) has 207 member countries.

These players are ready to learn how to play soccer like their heroes!

Goalkeeping shirts are usually long-sleeved to keep goalkeepers warm.

Soccer shirts should be loose enough to give you freedom of movement.

Goalkeepers sometimes wear sweatpants in the winter.

Socks should be pulled up to keep your shin pads in place.

Soccer Gear

If you want to learn how to play like a professional, you should start by getting the right kind of gear. Choosing gear is not about fashion. It is about safety, comfort, and flexibility. Your gear should fit properly, especially your cleats, so that you can move around the field as freely as possible.

Shin pads

Shins are easily injured so players protect them by wearing shin pads, even in practice. Shin pads are worn under soccer socks and also protect the ankle.

Cleats

Cleats are the most important part of your gear. Soccer cleats need to be flexible to allow all parts of your foot to move in any direction. They should also provide support and protection. To make sure you find the perfect fit, wear your soccer socks when you try on new cleats. Balance is an important part of soccer technique so the shoes have special cleats on the soles to keep players from slipping.

Astro shoes

For training and for games on artificial surfaces, players wear Astro shoes. These have lots of small pimples on the sole but do not have enough grip to wear on grass, except in dry conditions.

Goalkeepers' gear

Goalkeepers wear a slightly different gear than outfielders. They need more protection, especially when making diving saves. Goalkeeping shirts are usually long-sleeved and padded at the shoulders and elbows, while goalkeepers' shorts have extra padding to protect the hips.

Gloves

Goalkeepers wear gloves to protect their hands and give them extra grip on the ball. Gloves are made of strong but flexible materials such as latex so that goalkeepers' hands are able to move freely.

This is the view from the corner flag at Manchester United's home ground, Old Trafford.

The goal

One part of the field must always be the same size—the goal. Many years ago the size was set as eight feet high and eight yards wide, which in metric translates to 2.44 meters high and 7.32 meters wide.

The Field

You can play soccer anywhere—in your backyard, in the park, or on the school playground—but the best place for a safe and skillful game is on a special field. There are lots of different types of field, from natural surfaces such as grass to artificial surfaces which are great for indoor fields.

Mini field

Young players should not play on full-sized fields. Instead, they should concentrate on developing their techniques and game skills on special mini fields with smaller goals.

The long and short of it

Not all soccer fields are the same size. According to FIFA, the length of a field must be between 100 yards (90 meters) and 130 yards (120 meters) and the width not less than 50 yards (45 meters) and not more than 100 yards (90 meters). Of course, the length must always be greater than the width, otherwise the field would be square! Here are the key parts of the field:

1 Goal line
2 Goal
3 6-yard box
4 Penalty spot
5 18-yard box
6 Center spot
7 Center circle
8 Halfway line
9 Corner arc
10 Touch line

Balls

Soccer balls also come in different sizes. Young players should use smaller balls to help improve their technique.

Shall we dance?

This fun warm-up helps to develop balance, ball control, and coordination. The players are traveling forward and placing alternate feet on top of the ball. Next, the players have to do this while traveling backward!

Try to look where you are going, rather than at the ball.

Quickly bring the right foot down and put the left foot on the ball.

Warm-up

It is important for teenagers and adults to warm up and stretch their muscles before exercising. However, young players' bodies are more supple and flexible so they only need a general warm-up. The coach has developed fun ways of warming up the young players so that they are physically and mentally prepared for the game.

Throw, head, catch

It is reds versus blues and the object of the game is for one player to throw the ball, the next player to head it, and the third to catch it. It might sound easy, but this exercise requires teamwork, awareness, and determination.

Through the gate

A team must get the ball between two cones to score a point. This game helps the players get used to running with the ball and passing. To be successful they must work together.

The reds have scored a point!

Fast hands

The players throw five balls around in a circle, without dropping them. This tests coordination and communication. To make it even harder, the coach is timing them!

Passing

Players pass the ball so that their team keeps possession and moves toward the opposition's goal. A side foot pass (push pass) is perfect for short distances but has little power. A driven pass, using the laces (instep), is better for long distances.

Side foot pass

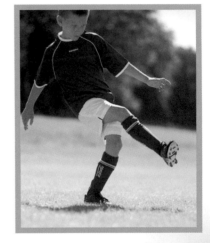

1 Place your nonkicking foot close to the side of the ball. Use your arms for balance and keep your eyes on the ball.

2 Swing your kicking leg back a short distance and strike the center of the ball with the side of your foot. Use your arms for balance.

3 Follow through with your kicking leg to generate power. With this type of pass, the ball should stay on the ground.

Chip pass

A chip is a short pass that aims to go over your opponent's head and drop into the path of your teammate. Place your nonkicking foot next to the ball and strike the bottom of the ball upward with a short, stabbing action.

Point your toes downward and strike the base of the ball, with no follow through.

Driven pass

Place your nonkicking foot next to the ball. Swing your kicking leg back and bend it slightly so that your knee is over the ball. Point your toes downward and strike the center of the ball with your laces. Follow through with your kicking leg.

This pass is a great way to move the ball beyond an opponent or over a long distance.

Lean back slightly if you want to give the pass some height.

Use your arms to help you balance.

The approach is the same as for a side foot pass.

Striking the ball with your laces generates more power.

Long lofted kick

1 To kick the ball high and over a longer distance, stand behind the ball and take a run up. As you approach the ball, plant your nonkicking foot a little way from the ball and swing your kicking leg back.

2 Strike the bottom of the ball with your laces and follow through with your kicking foot.

Leaning back will help lift the ball and make it travel farther.

Try to plant your nonkicking foot a little way from the ball.

Point your toes downward as you prepare to strike the ball.

16

Kicking

By striking the ball with different parts of your foot, you can make it go almost anywhere you want. Good kicking technique will help you master more advanced skills, so start with the two basic kicking techniques.

TOP TIPS

• Few players are naturally two-footed, so don't worry if one foot is stronger.

• Practice hard with your weaker foot and it will gradually improve.

Inside foot

Place your nonkicking foot next to the ball. Turn your kicking foot outward and strike the center of the ball with the inside of your foot.

Outside foot

Stand at an angle with your feet apart and your nonkicking foot behind. Strike the center of the ball with the outside of your foot.

Bending the ball

To make the ball bend you need to kick it off-center on the opposite side to the direction you want it to go. So, if you want to swerve the ball to the left, strike it on the right, and if you want to bend the ball to the right, strike it on the left. Using the inside of your foot bends the ball inward and using the outside of your foot bends the ball outward.

STAR PRO

England's **David Beckham** is perfectly poised to provide control, direction, and power to a right-wing cross. He is also famous for his ability to bend free kicks around the wall and into the top corner of the goal.

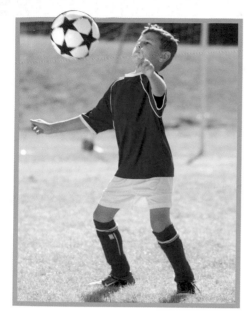

Ball Control

Being able to get the ball under control with your first touch will help your all-around game. The approach is the same, whether you control the ball with your head, chest, thigh, or foot—keep your eyes on the ball and move your body in line with the flight of the ball. With practice, you can learn to receive the ball at any height.

Chest control

Extend your arms, for balance, and to keep them away from the ball. Keep your body relaxed and arch your back slightly. As the ball hits your chest, move your shoulders forward so that the ball drops gently downward.

Side foot

Turn your foot to the side and, as it comes into contact with the ball, gently withdraw it to reduce the pace of the ball. Now try the same thing with the outside of your foot!

Laces

Great players can use their laces to control the ball. Bring your laces up to meet the ball and at the moment of impact bring your foot (and the ball) to the ground.

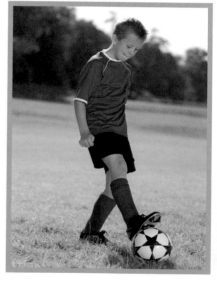

The wedge

As the ball comes toward you, lift your foot up and trap it between the sole of your foot and the ground. This technique brings the ball to a complete stop.

Thigh

Lean back slightly and use your arms for balance. Bend your standing leg a little and get your thigh in line with the ball. As the ball drops toward you, relax your thigh so that it forms a soft cushion and the ball drops downward.

Don't lean back too much—it might make you lose your balance!

Use your thigh when the ball is too high to control with your foot or too low to control with your chest.

STAR PRO

With practice, any player can master ball control. Here, Spanish striker **Fernando Morientes** has remarkably light control for a player of his height and strength.

Heading

During a game the ball is not always played to your feet, so you will often need to use your head to pass, control, clear, or score. Heading is a key technique, and it is important that you learn how to do it safely and effectively.

TOP TIP

Head the ball with the middle of your forehead. Never use the top or side of your head, since it will be painful, dangerous, and also less accurate.

Heading stance

There are three types of header, but they all start from the same basic position. As the ball comes toward you, plant your feet firmly on the ground. Keep your eyes on the ball and relax your body.

Basic header

Lean back a little so that your head and body are slightly behind the ball. Use your feet to push off and strike the ball with your forehead.

Defensive header

Push off from one foot and, as you jump, strike the bottom of the ball with your forehead. The ball should travel as far and as high as possible.

Attacking header

Strike the top or center of the ball with your forehead and aim it downward. This might create a goal-scoring chance for you or a teammate!

Remember to strike the ball with your forehead.

Keep your eyes on the ball.

Bend your knees for extra power.

STAR PRO

Italy's captain **Paolo Maldini** has played a record number of times for his country. He plays anywhere on defense. Here he soars commandingly above **Joahan Rodriguez** of Mexico to head the ball.

Dribbling practice

The best way to improve your dribbling skills is to practice. Line up some cones a few feet apart and dribble around them. The more you do it, the more skillful you will become. Soon you will be a confident dribbler!

Look up after every two or three touches.

Use the inside and outside of both feet!

See how fast you can go without losing control of the ball.

Dribbling

Dribbling is a way of moving the ball upfield. The player runs with the ball close to his or her feet and pushes it forward with lots of small, quick kicks. Dribbling is all about close control – without this a player will lose possession easily. The best dribblers are able to control the ball even in crowded goal areas.

Balance is an important part of dribbling. Good balance will allow you to change direction quickly, without losing control. You should use plenty of small kicks with the inside and outside of both feet plus the laces and try to look up, rather than at your feet.

Dribbling technique

1 Keep your body relaxed and try to look where you are going every so often, rather than just at your feet. Push the ball forward a short way using the inside of your foot.

2 Then use the outside of your foot to push the ball forward a little more. By alternating the inside, then outside of your foot, you will be able to dribble the ball in a straight line.

Outside hook

1 This is the opposite of the inside hook so right-footed players should have the ball on their right side and left-footed players should have it on their left. So, your kicking foot will be next to the ball. Plant your standing foot nice and wide.

2 Right-footed players will turn toward the right and left-footed players will turn toward the left. Use your standing leg as a pivot and swing your kicking leg. As the outside of your foot makes contact with the ball move your body and complete the turn. Bend your knees and race away in the opposite direction.

The standing leg helps you to balance and move into the turn.

Tackling

When the opposing team has the ball, you will need to regain possession. The most direct way of doing this is to make a tackle. You can either tackle a player from the front or the side. Tackles from behind are against the rules because they are dangerous and can cause serious injuries.

Block tackle

This is the most common type of tackle and it can be approached from the front or side. It can also be used for a 50-50 situation, which is when you and your opponent have an equal chance of gaining the ball.

Safe tackling

Every player should learn how to tackle, not just defenders. When making a tackle, keep your eyes on the ball. The key thing is timing—a mistimed tackle could cause injury to you or your opponent.

TOP TIPS

• Be committed—a clumsy or half-hearted tackle can cause injury and result in a penalty.

• Close down your opponent's space—you just might force them into making an error without even needing to make a tackle!

e to your
nd put her
Timing is
ait until
ass the
ck it
aking

2 Move forward and use the inside of your foot to make the tackle. Try to keep your eyes on the ball. If the ball becomes stuck between your feet, get your foot underneath and lift the ball away.

Turning

In tight situations a player will often have to change direction to avoid an opponent and create space. Turning requires skill, control, and balance so you need lots of practice. There are five basic turns shown in the book.

Drag back

This turn is for getting past defenders. Put your foot on top of the ball. Keep your eyes on the ball and drag it behind you. Then race away in the other direction, leaving the defender behind!

Inside hook

1 If you are right-footed, the ball should be on your left side and, if you are left-footed, the ball should be on your right side. Plant your standing foot close to the ball.

2 Using your standing leg as a pivot, swing your kicking foot around. (Right-footed players will turn from right to left and left-footed players will turn from left to right.)

3 As your body begins to move around, make contact with the ball using the inside of your foot and complete the turn. In a match situation this will happen fast!

Expert Turns

When you have mastered the drag back and the inside and outside hooks, it is time to move on to the two most difficult turns!

Stop turn

1 This turn is a great way of changing direction fast. As you are running with the ball, suddenly place your foot on top, to stop it dead.

2 Your defender will be surprised and will continue to run past you. While you have the advantage, carefully step over the ball.

3 After you have stepped over the ball, turn and take the ball in the opposite direction. Don't try and turn too fast or you will fall over!

The Cruyff turn

STAR PRO

As captain of Holland in the 1974 World Cup, **Johan Cruyff** was a master of the art of turning with speed and agility. His signature turn is still used today.

1 The key to this turn is convincing the opposition that you are about to pass the ball. Point to where you are pretending to pass.

2 Keeping up the act, plant your standing foot close to the ball. Pretend that you are going to use the other foot to pass.

3 At the last moment, use your kicking foot to flick the ball behind you. The opposition player will not be expecting this!

Keep your eyes on the ball.

Use your arms for balance.

STAR PRO

Portugal's **Cristiano Ronaldo** uses his pace and delicate ski[ll] to change direction, confus[e] defender, and create spac[e] himself or a teammate.

1 Get in clo[se] opponent a[nd] under pressure [is] important, so w[hen] she is about to p[ass] ball or try to kno[ck the] ball past you before m[aking] the tackle.

Sliding tackle

This type of tackle aims to clear the ball away from your opponent rather than to gain possession. Like the block, it can be from the front or the side but NEVER from behind. Time your tackle so that you slide in just as your opponent is about to pass or shoot. As you run toward your opponent, bend your nonkicking leg and then use your laces to push the ball away.

Use your arm and elbow to cushion your fall.

Be careful not to make contact with your opponent, since this may injure them or give away a free kick.

Slide in low and try to get your leg around the ball to hook it away.

Keep your eyes on the ball!

Swerve

To add swerve to a shot, you need to cut across the ball rather than striking the center. (See p. 17 for how to bend the ball in different directions.) Approach the ball from an angle and plant your standing foot a short distance from the ball. Strike the ball with the inside or outside of your foot and follow through.

This shot needs good balance.

Strike across the back of the ball to make it bend.

STAR PRO

Dutch striker **Ruud Van Nistelrooy** keeps his leg, body, and head in perfect alignment as he swerves the ball past the defender and toward the goal.

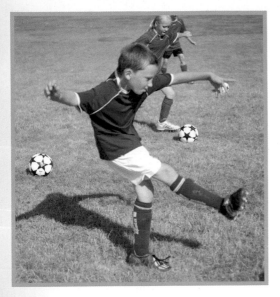

Shooting

Goals are what soccer is all about! To score a goal, a player can strike the ball in a number of ways and the technique is very similar to those used for passing (see p. 14–15) and kicking (see p. 16–17). Different parts of your foot alter the angle and power of the shot.

Shooting pratice

Line up some balls and take turns trying different types of shot. Every player should learn how to strike the ball, even defenders. In a game situation anything could happen, so wherever you play, you need to be able to shoot if a goal-scoring opportunity comes your way!

(see p. 14–15) and kicking (see p. 16–17).

TOP TIPS

• Keep your head still when striking the ball.

• To stop the ball from rising too much, keep your weight over the ball, not behind it.

Side foot

The simplest way to shoot is with the inside or outside of your foot. This type of shot is best for close range, when accuracy is more important than power. It is a great way of scoring when you have created space and only have the goalkeeper to beat.

Laces

The basics are the same as the driven pass (see p. 15) but the shot is quicker and more powerful. Use your non-striking foot for balance and swing your striking leg back. Strike the ball hard and fast with your laces and follow through powerfully.

Chip

If you see the goalkeeper too far off the goal line, you can try a chip shot. (See p. 14.) Point your foot down and aim for the underside of the ball. Lean backward, strike the ball with a sharp, stabbing action and do not follow through.

Sharp Shooting

It's fantastic when your team wins and even better if you score a goal! Here are some of the most crowd-pleasing ways of scoring goals, but be warned—even some of the world's top players find them difficult. Just relax, have fun, and see what you can do.

Overhead kick

1 This shot works when you have your back to the goal. Get in line with the ball and jump, using your nonkicking leg to propel you up. As you start to fall backward, quickly bring your kicking foot up.

2 Strike the back of the ball when your upper body is almost horizontal to the ground. Your nonkicking foot should be on the ground. This scissor action with your legs gives the shot power.

3 As you fall, stretch out your hand to soften the impact. Try to fall sideways and use your arms to cushion your fall. It is best to practice this technique on soft ground to prevent injury!

Which shot?

The type of shot you use depends on how the ball is coming toward you, the angle between you and the goal, and the position of the defenders. In a game, you might only have a split second to decide which shot to use, so quick thinking and good technique are vital.

Volleying

To hit a volley you need power, accuracy, and balance. It involves striking a ball when it is in the air, which is not as easy as it looks!

Side volley

Stand sideways to the goal and use your nonkicking leg to balance. Drop your leading shoulder and point your kicking foot. Using your standing leg as a pivot, swing your foot across your body, and strike back of the ball with your laces.

Keep your eyes on the ball at all times!

Front volley

If the ball arrives from the front, position your nonkicking foot behind the ball. As it approaches, raise the knee of your kicking leg and extend the ankle. Use your shoe laces to strike halfway down the back of the ball.

Extend your leg for the follow through.

2 Bend your front knee and get down low to the ground. Bring your arm forward and release the ball when it is level with your front foot. Rolling is a great way of turning defense into attack!

Rolling the ball

1 This underarm technique is only suitable for short distances because it doesn't generate much power. Hold the ball in the palm of your strongest hand and step forward with your opposite leg.

The leg opposite from your throwing arm should be forward.

Overarm throw

1 An overarm throw is a good way of starting a quick counterattack. Stand sideways and put the palm of your throwing hand behind the ball. Use your other arm to point at the target.

2 Place your opposite leg forward and bring your throwing arm over your shoulder. Release the ball at head height. Follow through until your throwing arm is extended.

Goalkeeping

Goalkeepers are more than just the last line of defense. A good goalkeeper is the backbone of the team. In addition to saving goals, he can launch attacking moves. A goalkeeper should be strong, athletic, and able to read the game.

Goal kick

1 With both hands, hold the ball out in front of you at about waist height. Keep your eyes on the ball. Take a few quick steps and release the ball.

2 Swing your kicking leg back and strike the bottom half of the ball with your laces. Follow through with your kicking leg for maximum power.

Diving saves

Goalkeepers need to be brave and have quick reactions. If the ball comes in low you will need to dive to keep it out of the net. Bend the knee nearest to where you will be diving and start to fall to that side. Collapse your leading leg and stretch your arms out in front of you. Get your hands behind the ball and try to catch it.

Keep your eyes on the ball at all times.

If you can't catch the ball, push it as far away as possible.

Get back on your feet as quickly as possible and be ready to make another save.

Be ready to dive as soon as the striker shapes up to shoot.

STAR PRO

Good footwork and sharp reflexes enable **Oliver Kahn** of Germany to get both hands on the ball as he dives to save. He will be able to bring the ball safely into his chest.

Hands-On Saves

In some ways, learning how to be a goalkeeper is more difficult than learning to be an outfield player. After all, goalkeepers need strong hands as well as skillful feet. A goalkeeper also needs to be calm under pressure and able to choose the best technique for the situation he is in.

Catching balls at chest height and above

Clench each hand into a fist with your thumbs on top.

1 Stretch your arms and get your hands behind the ball. Spread your fingers wide with your thumbs close together to form a "w" shape.

2 As the ball comes toward you hold the "w" shape and keep your hands relaxed. Catch the ball and then clutch it safely to your chest.

Punching

If you are unable to catch a cross, you will need to punch the ball clear instead. Put your clenched hands together and keep your wrists strong. Aim for the bottom half of the ball and punch it hard to get height and distance in your clearance.

TOP TIP

Be alert and always keep your eyes on the game. When you make a save, keep your head still and your body weight forward.

Cup and scoop

If a ball comes towards you between chest and knee height bend your knees, turn your palms upwards and **cup** the ball towards your body. If the ball comes towards you at a lower height bend down low, stretch out your arms with the palms up and gather or **scoop** the ball.

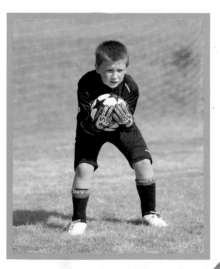

Practice Drills

When you have learned the basic techniques it is important that you keep practicing them. Here are some group drills to try in your next practice session. They are a fun way of testing how well you remember what you have learned and they also help you to get used to playing under pressure!

Attack and defense drill

This drill requires speed, control, and awareness. Each player has a ball and the object is to kick the other players' balls away while keeping possession of your own. You will need to use your tackling technique to rob the other players of possession, but at the same time you must dribble and turn to keep from losing your ball. This drill tests not only your dribbling, tackling, and turning, but also helps you to start thinking tactically.

Flag soccer

This is like traditional flag football, with a soccer twist. Each player has a ball at his feet and a flag tucked into the back of his shorts. The object is to grab as many flags as you can without losing your own. You must also keep your ball under control!

This drill is all about balance, control, and awareness. You also need to time your grab just right!

Star drill

This drill can be used to practice just about any technique! Arrange some cones in a circle (one for each player) and place one cone in the middle. Each player stands by a cone with a ball at her feet. The coach gives each technique a number. When he shouts that number the players have to move toward the center cone, doing the technique.

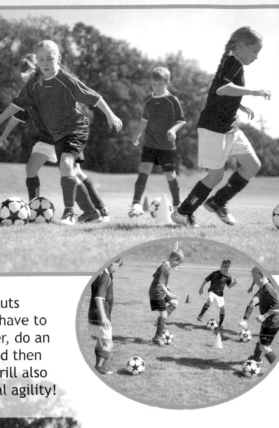

When the coach shouts "four!" the players have to dribble to the center, do an inside hook turn, and then dribble back. This drill also tests players' mental agility!

Shark attack!

Each player has a ball, except one. He is the "shark" and must try to steal the balls from all the other players. For most players this drill is about keeping possession, but the "shark" is on the attack and must use well timed tackles to acquire the ball. Players should take turns being the "shark."

Basic Laws

The game of soccer has seventeen laws that are constantly being revised and updated. Soccer laws are mostly just common sense and are about playing fairly, safely, and respectfully. Here are some important laws to remember.

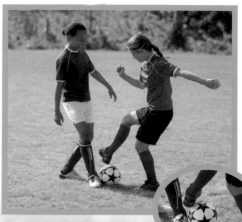

Foot over the ball

This is a foul tackle. A player's foot is not allowed to go over the top of the ball, since this could cause injury to an opponent.

Offside is judged from the moment the ball is played, not from when it is received.

TOP TIPS

• A player is only offside if he or she is involved in active play.

• The ball must be played forward for a player to be offside—sideways or backward are allowed.

• You cannot be offside in your own half or if an opponent plays the ball to you.

Tackle from behind

This is also a foul tackle. Tackles from behind are dangerous and often result in injury to the player and a red card for the tackler.

Handball

Only the goalkeeper is allowed to touch the ball with his hands in open play. If a defender does this in his penalty area he is likely to be given a red card.

OFFICIALS

The referee is the person in charge of the game. He ensures that the game is played according to the laws of soccer. He is supported by two assistants, one on each touch line.

Fouls and infringements usually result in a free kick for the opposition. For persistent breaches of the laws, the referee shows a yellow card. If a player receives two yellow cards in a game he will be sent off the field. Serious fouls result in a red card and a player must leave the field immediately.

The offside rule

This rule is designed to prevent attackers from goal-hanging. The rule is that a player must not be in front of the last defender when the ball is played to them.

Onside

Staying onside is about timing. The red attacker is in line with the blue defenders. He must not move past them until his teammate has played the ball.

Offside

The red attacker has moved too early! He is now beyond the last defender and therefore will be offside when the ball is played.

Attacking Skills

Learning correct techniques is only part of what you need to do to be a good player—you also need to learn how to perform well in a game situation. This means being able to work as part of a team and also being able to use your techniques under pressure. Here are some attacking game skills.

STAR PRO

Determination, strength, and great technique drive **Wayne Rooney** past two defenders and toward the goal for England.

The takeover

These players are practicing a pass called a takeover. It is a way of changing direction quickly. As one player dribbles, her teammate runs toward her. As he gets closer, she pushes the ball forward a little way. The other player takes the ball and dribbles away in the other direction.

One-two or wall pass

1 This is a simple but effective way to get through the defense. It requires teamwork and good communication (both verbal and nonverbal). Instead of trying to dribble past your opponent, send a short pass to the feet of a teammate.

The defenders are holding the line, hoping to catch the blue attacker offside.

This defender is trying to put pressure on the player with the ball.

Losing your defender

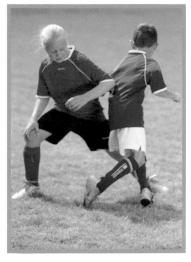

To get past defenders, adopt a sprinting stance—keep your body position low and bend your knees. Then you will be able to turn on a sudden burst of speed and leave the defenders trailing in your wake!

1 It can be hard to gain possession if you are being closely guarded so here is a way of losing your defender. As your teammate moves to pass the ball, pretend to move.

2 As the defender follows you, quickly change direction. If you do this quickly enough, your defender will be fooled and you will be free to receive the pass.

This attacker knows that she must stay onside if the move is going to work.

2 Continue to run forward, past the defenders. Shout to your teammate to make her aware of your run.

3 Your teammate should quickly pass the ball directly into your path, giving you the opportunity to race away.

The dummy

The angle of your body is very important.

1 This is a simple way of fooling your opponent. As the defender approaches, angle your body as if you are going to pass the ball with the inside of your foot.

2 The defender will move in the direction you are pretending to go. When she is fully committed, move your foot around the ball and use the outside of your foot to take the ball away in the opposite direction!

The defender is fooled!

3 You are now free to dribble the ball away. By the time the defender realizes she has gone the wrong way you will be long gone.

One-on-One Attack

The nutmeg

Attackers need to be confident on the ball and willing to take on defenders. With skill and clever play, you can create a goal-scoring opportunity for you or a teammate out of nothing. Here are a few skillful ways of getting past your opponent.

1 Only confident players should attempt this bold move. As the defender comes toward you, knock the ball through his legs.

2 Run past the defender and retrieve the ball. This works only if a defender is not concentrating, so don't try it too often!

TOP TIPS

• The key skills needed for getting past an opponent are speed and confidence.

• Be bold—use your techniques, knowing that you can beat defenders one on one.

STAR PRO

The strength and pace of the Ivory Coast's **Didier Drogba** ensures that his full body shields the ball from a despairing defender.

Step over

1 You need two skillful feet for this. As the defender approaches, pretend that you are about to pass the ball with the outside of one foot. Instead of passing, step all the way over the ball.

2 The defender will think you are going to pass and follow the direction of your foot. So you can simply use the outside of your other foot and race off in the opposite direction!

Defending Skills

Being a good defender is not just about making tackles. Defenders need to have good communication, awareness, and technique. They must also try to break down attacks by reading the game and putting attackers under pressure.

Intercepting a pass

1 This is a simple way of getting the ball without making a tackle. The reds are on the attack. As the blues close down the space, the red attacker prepares to pass the ball.

2 As the red attacker passes, the blue defender reads the pass and intercepts it. The blues have put pressure on the reds, read the game, and gained possession of the ball.

Zonal guarding
This system of guarding is not widely used but is an interesting alternative to man-on-man guarding. The blues have divided the penalty area into zones. Each defender, including the goalkeeper, guards his own zone instead of an individual player. In this system the defenders focus on the ball rather than on the opposing attackers.

At set pieces the defenders stand goal side.

This defender must keep her eyes on the ball and the red attacker!

The attacker will try and lose his guarder.

Man-on-man

This is the most common type of defending, or marking. Defenders guard an individual attacker for the whole game. The defender must be aware of what the attacker is doing at all times, even when he doesn't have the ball. So don't get caught out just watching the ball!

STAR PRO

French defensive midfielder **Claude Makelele** (left) uses all his experience to get ahead of an opposing forward and force him away from the penalty area danger zone.

Team Defending

Teamwork is a key part of effective defending. Aside from the goalkeeper, the defense is what stands in the way of the opposition scoring goals. Intelligent positioning and playing as a coordinated defensive unit are vital game skills to learn.

TOP TIP

Practice defending drills with your teammates to build up your understanding and communication. You should see a big improvement on game day.

Defending a corner

The reds have a corner. If the blues get their positioning right, the reds have less chance of scoring. Each red attacker is being closely guarded by a blue defender. The defenders stand between the attackers and the goal, watching the flight of the ball while also making sure the attackers don't make a sneaky move away from them. There are also two extra defenders guarding each goal post.

Offside trap

1 A well organized defense can also work together to catch the attackers offside. The defense stands in a line as the attacker is about to pass the ball to her teammate. At this point, the red attacker without the ball is onside.

2 Just as the attacker is about to pass the ball, the blue defenders all take a step forward in a line. Then, as the ball is played they raise their arms to show that the red attacker is offside. The blues have used teamwork to win a free kick.

Defending a free kick

When the attackers have a free kick within shooting distance, the best way to defend is to organize a wall. The goalkeeper positions a line of defenders so that it blocks the attackers' view of the near post. The goalkeeper then covers the far post, making it harder for the attacker to score.

The goalkeeper should have a clear view of the ball.

Make sure that the wall stands firm!

STAR PROS

Germany organizes a five-man wall to defend a free kick. Usually the goalkeeper and the player closest to the ball organize the position of the wall.

49

STAR PRO

Czech goalkeeper **Petr Cech** goes all out to make a save. His hands, arms, and body are behind the line of the ball.

Aim for height and distance.

Goalkeepers have to be brave under pressure!

High balls

If the ball is in the air, it is difficult to catch it cleanly, especially if an attacker is putting you under pressure. Goalkeepers need to be brave and confident in these situations. Just keep your eyes on the ball and try to punch the ball away as high and as far as possible.

Goalkeeper in Action

In a game, goalkeepers need to be able to react under pressure. Often the goalkeeper is the only player standing between the opposition and a surefire goal—if she makes a brilliant save she will be a hero, but if she makes a mistake it could prove very costly for the team.

TOP TIP

Penalties favor the attacker—if they strike the ball into the corners, they will probably score. So, when you are practicing penalties, forget about the corners! Mark out a smaller goal with cones and practice making saves in this area.

Penalties

1 Every goalkeeper has a different idea about the best way to save a penalty, but here are the basics. Before the attacker strikes the ball, focus your mind on what you are about to do. You should try to ignore any crowd noise.

2 Goalkeepers usually decide which way they are going to dive before the ball has been struck. If you guess right, you stand a good chance of saving the penalty. But remember, a well struck penalty is almost impossible to save!

Narrowing the angle

1 If you are faced with a one-on-one situation with a striker, you need to make it harder for them to score.

2 Come out of the goal and move forward in line with the ball. This gives the striker less space to shoot and blocks his view of the goal.

51

The Dead Ball

When the ball has gone out of play or the referee has stopped for a foul or infringement, it is known as a dead ball. You should practice these situations with your teammates so that you can make the most of these opportunities in a game.

Throw in

1 Throw ins are awarded when the opposition kick the ball over the touch line. To start, position your feet on or behind the touch line.

2 Hold the ball behind your head, with both hands. Bring it forward quickly and release it before it is level with your head.

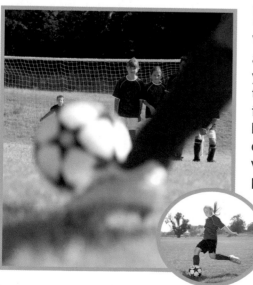

Free kick

When the referee awards a free kick, he will tell you where it should be taken and when to take it. If it is a direct free kick within scoring distance, the opposition will set up a wall (see p. 49). In that case, you need to bend the ball (see p. 17) around the wall or chip it (see p. 14, p. 32) over the top.

Penalty

A penalty is great chance to score, but it is also a high-pressure situation. Try to stay calm and choose your spot before you strike the ball.

Taking a corner

A corner kick is awarded if the opposition knocks the ball over their own goal line. The corner must be taken from the corner arc on the same side of the field that the ball crossed the goal line. A corner is often a great opportunity to score a headed goal, so it is good idea for the tallest players to come forward.

The whole of the ball must be inside the area known as the corner arc.

The opposition must be at least 10 yards (9.1 meters) away.

Short corner

You could try a short corner for variation. Instead of playing a long ball to the near or far post, make a short pass to your teammate. He can either cross the ball in or pass it back to you so that you can make a run into the penalty area.

Try to aim the ball at the near or far posts as they are difficult areas to defend.

It is possible to score directly from a corner!

Tricks of the Trade

Professional players have such great technique that they are often able to dazzle the crowds (and surprise the opposition) with amazing displays of skill. Try some of these tricks and you will be a superstar show-off in no time!

Quick flick

Put the ball between your feet. Jump and flick the ball up behind you. Then turn and volley the ball. You should work on this move in practice before you try it in a game.

STAR PRO

Brazil's World Cup inspiration **Ronaldo** demonstrates balance and clever footwork as he conjures up a sly trick to unbalance two Argentine defenders. A trick like this requires great technique and a lot of confidence!

Balance

This trick is only for the purpose of showing off. Try balancing the ball on your head or shoulders—it is much harder than it looks!

STAR PRO

Sweden's **Freddie Ljungberg** could use a safety net as he launches himself into a spectacular overhead move. He makes this difficult shot look effortless. See p. 32 for a step-by-step guide to overhead kicks.

Juggling in this position requires a lot of ball control because you can only move your feet!

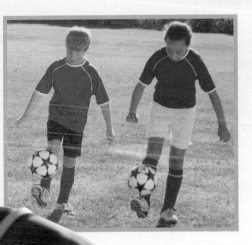

Juggling

They look impressive and are a great way of practicing ball control (see p. 18-19). Use your feet and thighs to prevent the ball from touching the ground. Try to stay relaxed.

TOP TIPS

Only attempt a trick in a game if you feel confident and be prepared to look a little foolish if it doesn't work out!

The Game

Playing in a game is a great way to test how much you have learned! You must try to remember everything that the coach has taught you so that you play well as part of the team.

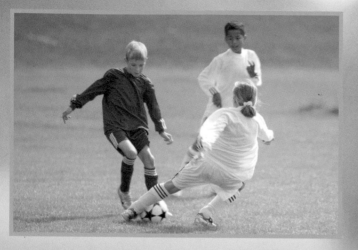

The goalkeeper should always be ready for action!

Turning on the skill

As the red player prepares to make a tackle, the white player uses the techniques she has learned to go past him. With a great piece of skill, she executes an inside hook turn (see p. 25).

Awareness

Who wants the ball? The red team has a free kick but there is no one to pass to!

Corner

The reds are defending the goal well, but the whites need to bring more players forward.

Goal?

The attacker has only the goalkeeper to beat. His body position is excellent as he shapes up to shoot. He is going to strike the ball with his laces (see p. 31) and if he swerves the shot to the left, the goalkeeper will surely be beaten.

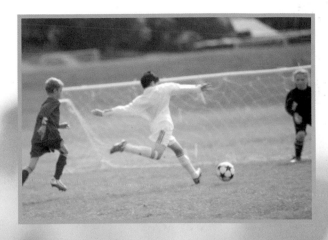

Skills in action

The red player has noticed her teammate on the edge of the penalty area. She tries to aim her driven pass (see p. 15) right into his path. This is a great example of vision.

Close control

The white player has controlled the ball very well (see p. 18-19). Her teammate is telling her that he wants to receive the pass, but the white player may choose to go on herself.

50-50

This ball could go either way as both players try their hardest to get to it first. Both players are determined!

STAR PRO

Ronaldinho of Brazil is described by the Dutch coach Frank Rijkaard as "the player who has absolutely everything." In 2005 he won the FIFA World Player of the Year and was also named European Footballer of the Year.

Keep practicing

Even the best players in the world have to practice. Technique can always be improved and new skills learned. Remember to keep training both feet and your weaker foot will gradually become stronger.

The Future

Now that you have learned how to play soccer like a star professional, the next step is to join a team and keep playing the game. Your technique will continue to improve with regular coaching sessions and by playing in competitive games. It is also a great way to keep your body fit and active.

The FIFA World Cup

Every player dreams of playing in the World Cup Finals. The competition has taken place every four years since 1930 and is a chance for the best teams to shine in front of the whole world. It is an inspirational occasion for everyone.

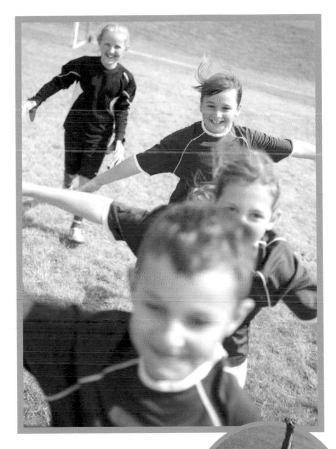

STAR TEAM

Greece triumphed against the odds at the European Championships in Portugal in 2004 thanks to tactical discipline, high fitness levels, and outstanding team spirit.

Have fun!

The best thing about soccer is that it can be played by people of any age, background, ability, race, or sex. So there's no excuse not to get out there and start playing!

Glossary

A

Astro shoes—soccer shoes with small studs on the soles, suitable for playing on artificial or firm surfaces.

C

Center spot—the point in the center of the field where the game starts and restarts after a goal.

Chip—a pass or shot in which the bottom of the ball is struck with a short stabbing motion with no follow through.

Cleats—special soccer shoes designed with studs (also called cleats) on the soles.

Corner arc—the area at the corner of the field where the corner kick is taken.

Corner flag—a flag marking the corner arc.

Corner kick—an attacking dead ball situation arising when the defending team puts the ball over its own goal line.

Cross—to kick or pass the ball across the field, usually into the penalty area to create a goal-scoring opportunity.

Cruyff turn—a deceptive turn named after the world-famous Dutch player of the 1970s, Johan Cruyff.

Cup—the technique a goalkeeper uses to catch a ball between chest and knee height.

D

Dead ball—a break in play, often due to a free kick or throw in.

Drag back—when a player drags the ball behind him and executes a quick turn and change of direction.

Dribble—moving the ball with lots of small, quick kicks, usually with both feet.

Driven pass—a powerful pass struck with the laces that can travel over a long distance.

Dummy—to pretend to pass or shoot in one direction to deceive an opponent and then to move the opposite way.

E

Eighteen-yard box—the larger marked area around the goal, in which a penalty may be given.

F

Far post—the goal post farthest away from the point of attack e.g. a corner or free kick.

Field—the area of play.

FIFA—the world of soccer's governing body, the Fédération Internationale de Football Association.

Foul—an infringement of the rules of soccer, such as when a player trips, kicks, or pushes an opponent (accidentally or deliberately).

Free kick—when play is stopped by the referee and a kick awarded to the opposing side, usually due to a foul or infringement.

G

Goal—1. The nets supported by two posts and a crossbar at each end of the field where the goalkeepers stand.
2. When the ball crosses the line into the goal area and a team scores.

Goal line—the line linking the corner flags with the goal posts.

Guard—to position yourself close to an opponent so that it is difficult for him or her to receive or pass the ball. This is also known as marking.

H

Halfway line—the line that separates one half of the field from the other.

Handball—a type of foul. It is illegal for an outfield player to touch the ball with his or her hand in open play.

I

Infringement—to break one of the rules of soccer.

Instep—the upper surface of the foot or cleat, also called the laces.

Intercept—to steal possession of or get in the way of an opponent's pass.

L

Laces—the upper surface of the foot or cleat, also called the instep.

Long lofted kick—a powerful kick using

the laces that rises above the ground.

M
Match—a competitive game, usually comprising two halves of 45 minutes.
Mini field—a small field, especially for young players.

N
Near post—the goal post nearest to the point of attack, such as a corner or free kick.
Nutmeg—to kick the ball through an opponent's legs and then retrieve it on the other side.

O
Offside—when an attacker has moved beyond the last defender as the ball is played forward.
One-two—a quick back-and-forth pass between two players, also known as a wall pass.

P
Penalty—a specific kind of free kick awarded when an attacker is fouled in the penalty area.
Penalty spot—the place from where the penalty is taken.
Possession—to have the ball.
Punch—when the goalkeeper uses his or her fists to make a save.
Push pass—a short pass with the side of the foot, also known as a side foot pass.

R
Reading the game—playing the game intelligently, e.g. using tactical knowledge to improve positioning, passing, tackling, and intercepting.
Red card—a player is shown this after a particularly bad offense or after receiving two yellow cards in a game.
Referee—the official in charge of the game, who checks that the laws of soccer are not broken.
Referee's assistants—the flag-carrying officials positioned on each touchline who help the referee.

S
Scoop—the technique a goalkeeper uses to gather a ball below knee height.
Score—to get a goal.
Sent off—when a player receives a red card and is told to leave the field of play.
Shin pads—protective shields for the shins and ankles, usually worn underneath the socks.
Shoot—to aim a kick or pass at the goal.
Side foot pass—a short pass with the side of the foot, also known as a push pass.
Six-yard box—the small marked-out area around the goal.
Stop turn—a way of changing direction quickly by stopping the ball at speed.
Swerve—to kick or strike across the back of the ball so that it bends in the opposite direction.

T
Tackle—to challenge a player fairly for the ball. A tackle can be block or sliding.
Throw in—a throw from the touch line awarded by the referee when the opposition has kicked the ball out of play.
Touch lines—the two lines running down the length of the field.

U
Volley—to kick the ball before it touches the ground, usually as a goal shot.

W
Wall—a line of two or more players defending their goal against a free kick.
Wall pass—a quick back-and-forth pass between two players, also known as a one-two.
Wedge—to trap the ball under your foot to control it.

Y
Yellow card—this is shown by the referee for a serious offense or for persistent offending.

Index

LONDON, NEW YORK, MUNICH,
MELBOURNE, AND DELHI

Senior Art Editor   Guy Harvey
Senior Editor   Catherine Saunders
U.S. Editor   Margaret Parrish
Publishing Manager   Simon Beecroft
Brand Manager   Lisa Lanzarini
Category Publisher   Alex Allan
DTP Designers   Lauren Egan and Hanna Ländin
Production Controller   Amy Bennett
Coach and Technical Adviser   Mark Drabwell
Star Pro Panels   Keir Radnedge
Picture Researcher   Will Jones

First American Edition, 2006
Published in the United States by
DK Publishing, Inc.
375 Hudson Street, New York, New York, 10014
08 09 10 10 9 8 7 6 5 4
Copyright © 2006 Dorling Kindersley

ISBN-13 978-0-75662-032-5

Color reproduction by MDP Ltd., UK
Printed and bound in Italy by L.E.G.O.
Discover more at
www.dk.com

The Publisher would like
to thank the following
libraries for permission to
reproduce their images:
(b=bottom, c=center, l=left, r=right,
t=top)
Adrian DENNIS/AFP/Getty Images:
25tr. Alex Livesey/Getty Images: 59bl.
Alexander Hassenstein/Bongarts/Getty
Images: 49br. ANTONIO SIMOES/AFP/Getty
Images: 27tr. Ben Radford/Getty Images:
59tl. Christof Koepsel/Bongarts/Getty
Images: 30br. FRANCOIS XAVIER MARIT/AFP/
Getty Images: 36br; 50tl. FRANCK FIFE/
AFP/Getty Images: 47br. Jamie McDonald/
Allsport: 14br. JAVIER SORIANO/AFP/Getty
Images: 19br. © Karoly Arvai/Reuters/
Corbis: 55tr. KIM JAE-HWAN/AFP/Getty
Images: 28tl. Lars Baron/Bongarts/Getty
Images: 32br. Laurence Griffiths/Getty
Images: 21bl. Mary Evans Picture Library:
6cbl. Matthew Peters/Manchester United
via Getty Images: 42c. Mike Hewitt/Getty
Images: 45bl. MIGUEL ROJO/AFP/Getty
Images: 13cl. Shaun Botterill/Getty Images:
23c; 35cr; 52tr. © SPORTSPHOTO AGENCY/
CORBIS SYGMA: 10c. © Stockdisc Classic/
Alamy: 9br. Stuart Franklin/Bongarts/Getty
Images: 58tr. © Toby Melville/Reuters/
Corbis: 17br. VANDERLEI ALMEIDA/AFP/
Getty Images: 54bl.Vladimir Rys/Bongarts/
Getty Images: 41tr. Will Jones: 9tr.

The Publisher would like to thank the following young players
for making the photoshoot such great fun: Biyi Adetunji, Todd
Armstrong, Brooke Barfoot, Daniel Barnes, Bianca Bragg,
Louis Claridge, Niall Crouch, Tricia Gould, Morgan Hammond,
Jake Holmes, Sian Horrigan, Ashleigh James, Abigail Kemball Cook,
Ellie King, Niall McDonough, Michael McManamon, Ria Melvin,
Piero Monastero, Sabrina Monastero, Trai Sackett,
Bethany Stanfield, Beth Wood, and Charlie Young.